# i USED to BE AFRAID of ANIMALS

## KABVIKA KAMUNGA

illustrations by TRis BAiN

# I Used to be Afraid

Kabuika Kamunga

Published by 1st World Publishing
P.O. Box 2211, Fairfield, Iowa 52556
tel: 641-209-5000 • fax: 866-440-5234
web: www.1stworldpublishing.com

First Edition

LCCN: 2016909268

ISBN: 978-14218-3757-4

Illustrations: Tris Bain.

MY MOTHER ONCE FOUND A BOA IN OUR VEGETABLE GARDEN. i RAN AND HID IN MY BED. HOW DID THE LARGE SNAKE LEAVE THE RAINFOREST AND GET INTO OUR GARDEN? i DID NOT KNOW.

i DID NOT WANT TO KNOW. i STAYED UNDER THE COVERS UNTIL IT WAS GONE.

WE HAD A DOG. i WAS AFRAID OF HIM. i WOULD NOT GO OUTSIDE THE HOUSE AT NIGHT WHEN HE WAS FREE TO ROAM iN THE YARD.

HE HAD SHARP VAMPiRE TEETH.

I WAS AFRAID OF COCKROACHES.

THEY WERE BIG AND HARD WHEN I TOUCHED THEM BY ACCIDENT OR WHEN THEY FLEW INTO ME ON PURPOSE. I WOULD RUN OUT OF MY BEDROOM AND ASK MY YOUNGER BROTHER to get THEM out.

I ONCE VISITED A MAN WHO HAD A CROCODILE IN HIS SWIMMING POOL. I NEVER WENT TO VISIT HIM AGAIN.

i was afraid of every single animal.

Then i met the monkey named coco.

Coco was nice when my older sister was present. When she was not around, he liked to play pranks on me.

One day when i was playing in the back yard with my red ball, he jumped out from behind his tree and scratched my ankle.

i decided to get back at him. The next day, when coco wasn't looking, i snuck up behind him and pulled his tail.

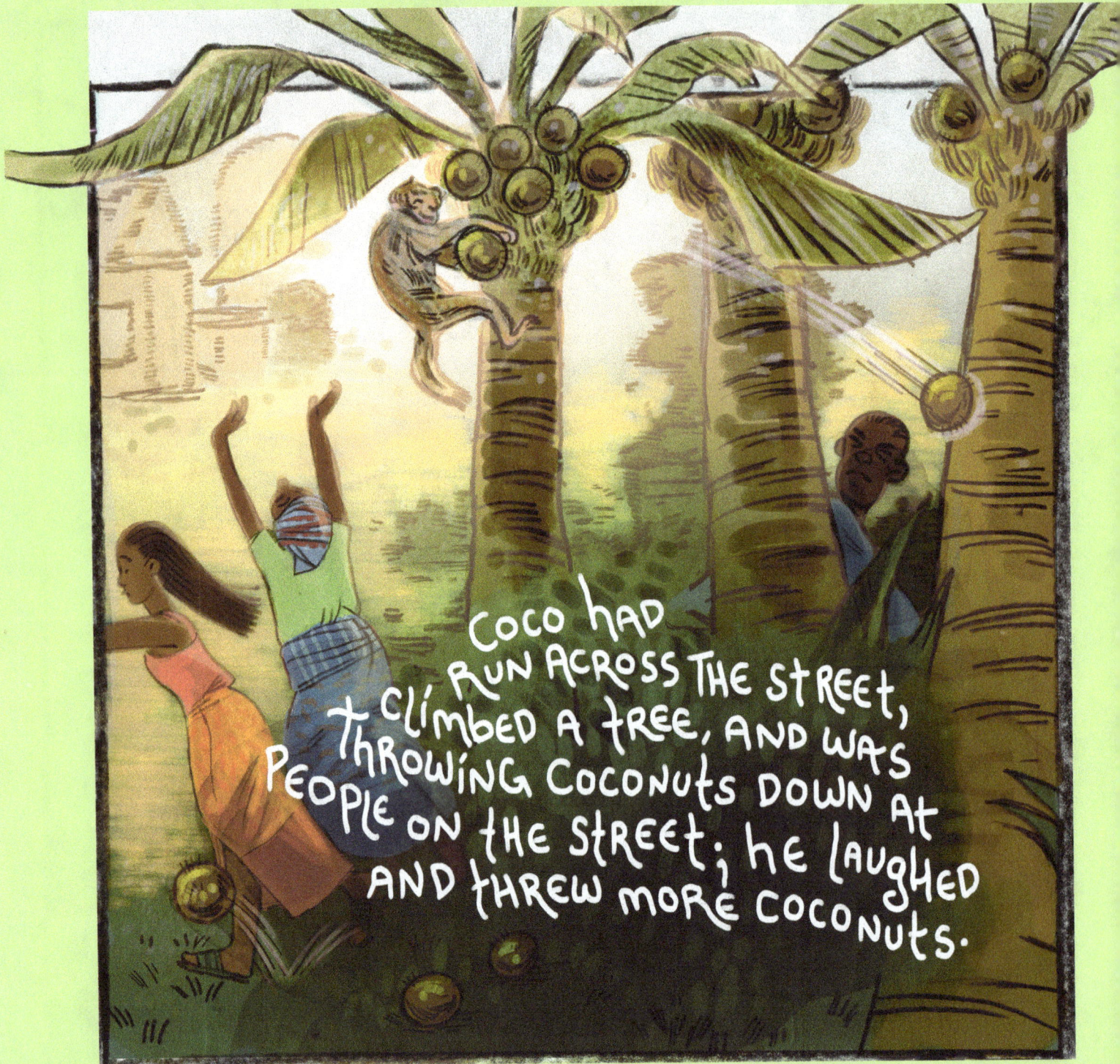

COCO HAD RUN ACROSS THE STREET, CLIMBED A TREE, AND WAS THROWING COCONUTS DOWN AT PEOPLE ON THE STREET; HE LAUGHED AND THREW MORE COCONUTS.

ONE TIME I WAS BABYSITTING MY BABY BROTHER WHO WAS CRYING NON-STOP. I DIDN'T KNOW WHAT TO DO.

When my family went on a long trip, I asked my sister. "Can we go home now? I miss Coco."

I realized then that I liked Coco, I just found him annoying sometimes.

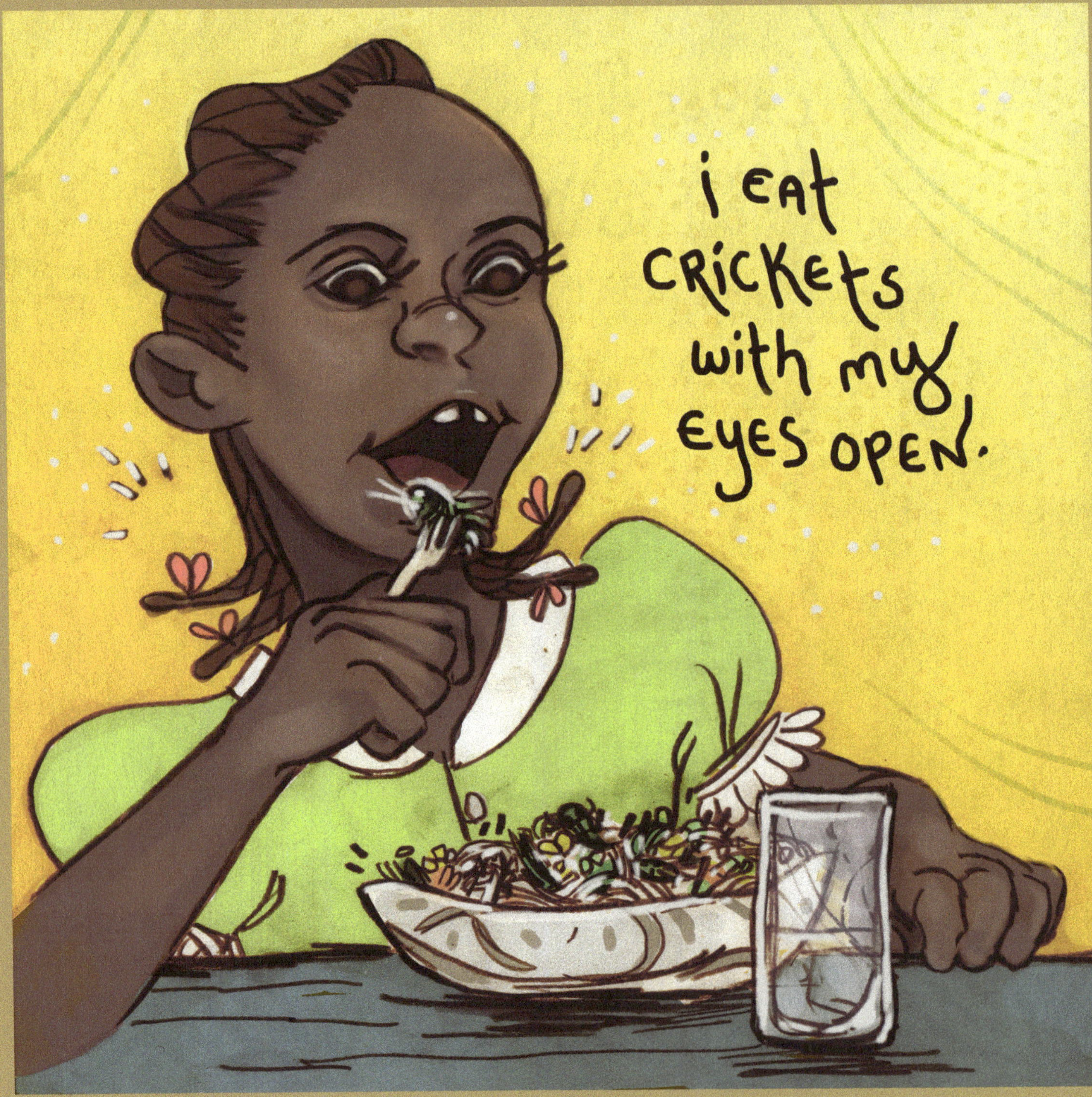
i eat crickets with my eyes open.

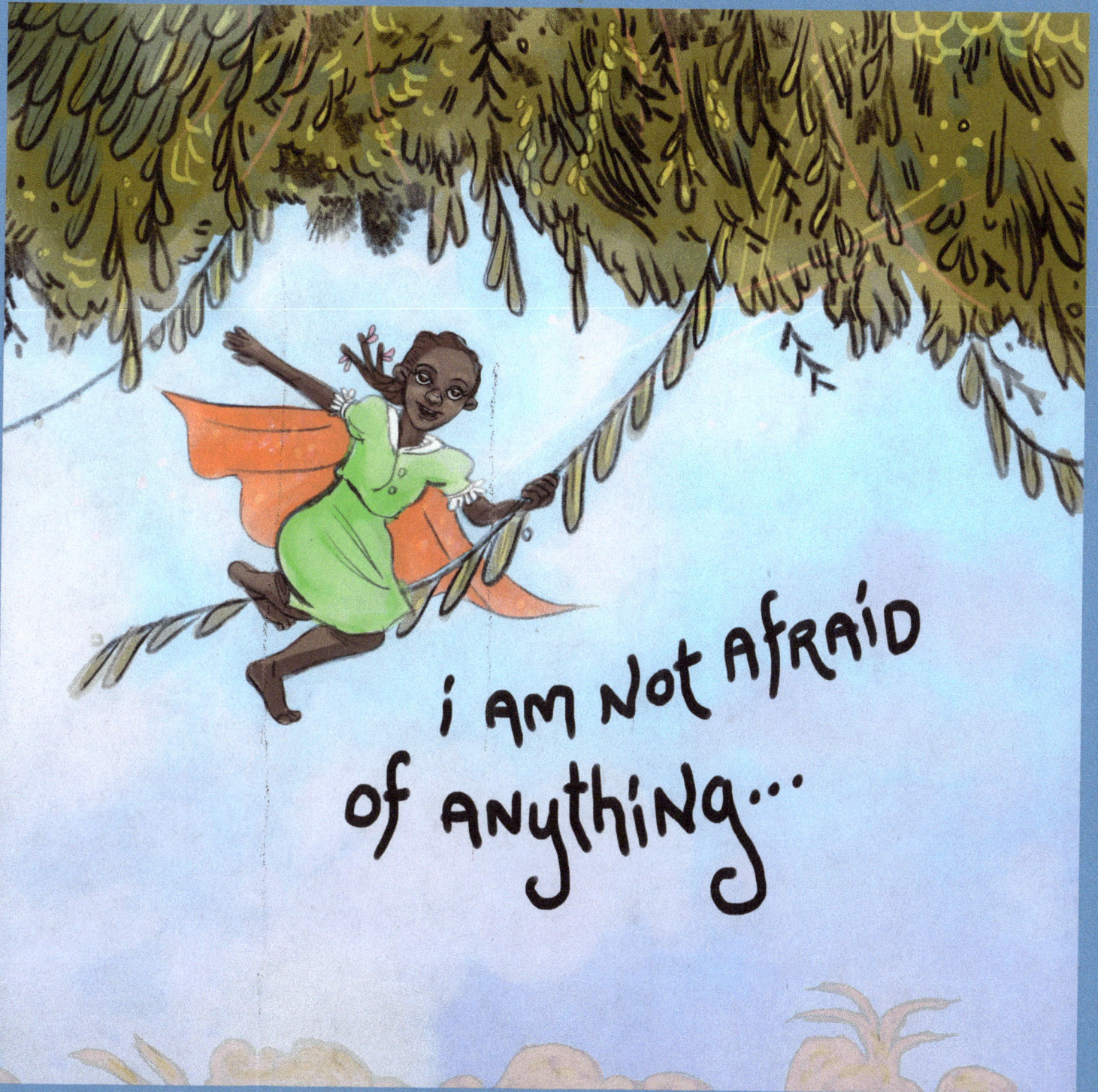

i am not afraid of anything...

... ok maybe
not anything.

the end

www.ingramcontent.com/pod-product-compliance
Lightning Source LLC
Chambersburg PA
CBHW080938040426

42443CB00015B/3472